nipê wânîn

my way back

nipê wânîn

my way back

Mika Lafond

thistledown press

Thistledown Press Ltd.
410 2nd Avenue North
Saskatoon, Saskatchewan, S7K 2C3
www.thistledownpress.com

Library and Archives Canada Cataloguing in Publication

Lafond, Mika
[My way back]
Nipê wânîn = My way back / Mika Lafond.
Text in original English and in Cree translation.

ISBN 978-1-77187-129-7 (softcover)

I. Title. II. Title: My way back.
PS8623.A35897M9 2017   C811'.6   C2017-901108-1

Author photo by Shelley Banks
Cover and book design by Jackie Forrie
Printed and bound in Canada

Canada Council   Conseil des Arts
for the Arts   du Canada

SASKATCHEWAN
ARTS BOARD

Canadä

Thistledown Press gratefully acknowledges the financial assistance of the Canada Council
for the Arts, the Saskatchewan Arts Board, and the Government of Canada for its publishing
program.

Acknowledgements

Grateful acknowledgement is made to the following publications in whose pages these poems first appeared: kimiwan zine, The *Malahat Review, Education Matters*. Thank you to Thistledown Press for the publication of this book.

This book would not have been possible without nôhkôm Gladys Wapass-Greyeyes sharing her time to be my teacher, and speaking the gift of nêhiyawêwin language with me. You have helped me find my way back. Thank you for your teachings and stories.

A very special thank you to my poetry mentors William (Bill) Robertson, Mary Maxwell and Jeanette Lynes for your guidance through the writing process of this book. For reading the first drafts of these poems, and giving me the feedback necessary to really make me reflect on what I wanted the poems to become.

To Rita Bouvier for your support of my work and your encouragement to see the words in new and insightful ways.

Thank you to Shelley Banks for the author photograph.

With great love and respect, thank you to my parents for your support and patience through all of the lessons of life that are written in this book.

Contents

For Kane and Emberlee

kicawâsimisinawak êkîmîkoyak mâmawiyôtawimaw
our children are a gift from the Creator

acâhk

Spirit

niya

ni nêwiyawan
askiy kîcikamihk—nipî ohcipayin—yotin kîsik—mîna iskotêw
pimâtisiwin niki kiyawan
tâpiskohc pîsih kistikanîs
nikaspowitaw

nikiskisin mîna âtayohkêmakan
itê êpêyohciyan

nikiki yawâmâwâk nitêhi kaki nîkân ohtawicik mîna kapê nokosicik
pêyak acâhkowin—âcimowihihk

nôhkom nikî mâmtonêyimik
oskîsikwâpo nikî pimâhokon nikî wîcêtamwan opawâtamowina
kiwêtinohk sâkâstênohk âpihtakisikanohk mîna pahkisimôtahk
nicâpanpanak ocêpîkwatamok askiy

kimihko—yapîna pimiciwaniyo kakêta wisiwin askiy iyinîsiwin

kâpîwan iyotik namôya nipêyakon
tapiskohc nipiys ka ayîtakwa ta mok mitosihk nimicimêyitên kakês
kwêwina mîna wâhkôtowin
kihtwam ta ohpikiw mîtos

namôya nipônayitin—nitacâhkowin

I am

I am four elements
dirt of earth—water of sea—wind in sky—fire of sun
I am matter—a cell—I am an organ of life
all life from one single cell reproduces
bearing blood of ancestors

I am a fraction of memory—a piece of history
a segment of the ones I come from

in my heart pumps the blood of my predecessor and my descendent
of one spirit—intertwined by story

I am my grandmother's thought
I was in her tears—I have shared dreams with her
I am a sprig of present produced by the past—cultivating the future
my great grandmothers are the roots planted deep
within this land stretching north and south—east and west

our blood—the sap that runs the trunk and rises towards the sky
saturates growth with life—with knowledge—with stories that
divide—flood—flow in rivers in our veins

I am a tiny leaf upon this tree—never alone in a bitter winter wind
but tied to branches of relationships and teachings
though my life is short—the seed of a tree will grow another

I am a spiritual being—I do not die

nipê wânîn

nitapin kaski-tipiska wâsisowak acâhkosak
ni mêskwâpimâwak kâkî nikâno-têcihk
kâkwa-tipiskâk sakicîcêntowak
kiwêtinohk ohci pêsâkiwê-simowak
nîpâmayatan ôskaskosiw akwahahowak-kîskasâkêwak

nicapân-panak—mîwêyitamwak ê-nîmihitocik

namôya nikiskêyitên kêyâpic nipêtawâwak
kitowêsinok yotinok mîna kwâmwâci tipiskahk
nicâpanpanak kânîmihitocik
      wîyawaw piko pêhtawêwak mistikwaskikwa
nikwamwatapin—wanahpitêmakan ni-mâmihtonêyicikan
tâpiskohc mihkwapimakwa—wânêhi-tamowin
kwâmawatastêw ocepihkosi

namôya nikiskêyitên kêyapic nipêtawâwâk
nipakitêyitên kikway namôya kwayask êspayik
nitacâhk nitohtam—nikiskisin
tawâpahtaman kâpê mihko-sâkîwêt-pîsim
yayâna askîtakoska-kikisimo maskosiya yotinohk

niwayinîtotamwân ospitona nôhkom—nitôkiskinwahamâkêm
êkâ pîkiskwê kinohkotân manâcisowin
cistêmaw mîyakaso ôpâpasiw—kispakapiw iskotê
nisikac mêstikasiw miyakaso
pêyatik pîkiskwânawiw okîci-twawiniwâw
namôya ki-kisîwêtotên
kâya sêkisi—wasakâpiwâk iskwêwak—niwâpamison—
nipênâtikwak
omihkowaw—nimihko nicâpanpanak

~ 14 ~

my way back

sitting under a black sky sprinkled with stars
my eyes are called to the ones who have gone before—
late at night they join hands—brilliant serpentine belt
in the northern sky
        purple splashes on green—shawl upon skirt

great grandmothers—my ancestors love to dance

I didn't know I could still hear them
swishing in the wind—in the solitude of dark
        great grandmothers who danced
        to a drum only they could hear
until I sit in silence—thoughts tangled
like red willow branches—confusion settling in the roots

I didn't know I could still hear them
until I fell away from chaos—my spirit listened—remembered
        to view a crimson sunrise—wonder at clouds etched with gold
        swim in the deep blues of sky—dance with grass in the wind

I find my way back to the arms of nôhkom
my grandmother—my teacher
she shows me silence is a sign of respect
        as tobacco burns in the shell—smoke rising—thick at the flame
        slowly dissipating—until it is scent in the air
words are spoken in hushed voices
their sacredness not to be shouted
        do not be afraid
        in a circle of women I see myself—they came before me
their blood is my blood—my ancestors

kâya pîkiskwê kinokotân manâcisiwin
isiwêpisiwina kâkî kwêskinên—ahkwan pêci nâway pakitêyita
kâhkiyaw kâki pônêyitamâkan
kisêwâtotâtowin—pêyakowimakan—kâhkiyaw iyiniwâk—pisis
iwâk—kâhkiyaw kîkway
nisîkac nipahkahokon nitachâk êhêw

wâsakâpiwâk iskwêwak êkôta nimiskâson

silence is a sign of respect—attitudes can be changed
     pain carried from the past—can be let go
     all can be forgiven
kisêwâtotatowin—one love—all people—all animals—all things
my heartbeat slows—my spirit breathes

in a circle of women I find myself

kihtwâm ka wâpamitin

sênapân-âpihtêyiw o-mâmitonêyicikan
kêsi yoskêka sênapânêkin—miyikôwisiw mihtêhi
    otina kânitawêyitaman—namôya îkisi namôya nohtaw

apihkatêw wîhkask mîyâkasikan
akwaskitinikô—o-kâkîsimôwin
    tâtipi ôpâpatêyiw

kihiwâk wîcêtowak—kêtê-skwêw itwêw
pênîtacowêpihawak waskasiwâwa ohci âyitinamwak
asocikêwina

nikî ayân nîsta pêyakwaw—asocikêwina ôtê nîkân

miskam pônêhitamâtowin
moskwêyitam—nisitohtam kakêskwêwin
tânispî kâyitina mîna tânispi tapakitina

niskisik-wâpoy ohci pakitâpawêw mîtâtamowin

nikî wîhik
niskiskwêw
okîci niska—hay hay
kâkiskihwahamawiyin
âtôtêwin—kêcinâhowin—maskikîw niska
    paskâpowin kwayaskakotêw
    maka mihtêhi kiskêyitam

kinêhiyâwin—kêtê-skwêw kîhtwam pîkiskwêw
kâpê sâkâstêk nanâskomoh
    nanahita kakêskwêwina

see you again

she is wrapped in ribbons of thought
– soft satin whispers—a gift to the heart
      takes what she needs—no more no less

braided curls of smudge
embrace her—gather her prayers
      upward in twisting smoke

eagles marry—old lady says
they dive clutching talons
together—a vow

I had that once—promise of a future

finding forgiveness
in midnight tears—a lesson
about when to hold on and when I need to let go

my tears brought freedom from regret

she named me
niskiskwêw—
noble goose—thank you
for your teachings
migration—loyalty—goose medicine
      blind eyes that fly straight
      because the heart knows

kinêhiyâwin—old lady speaks again
– at sunrise give thanks
      obedient to protocol

nitohta—listen
nika wihtamâk—nêwo kwêskâhitonah—pêyak wîyasôwêwin
kâya ayêciski—pêyatik pimohtê
    kaya êkosi itwêw
    goodbye

listen—nitohta
now she will tell me—four seasons—one law
do not leave footprints—walk softly
      don't say
      goodbye

sipwêtêyani

mistikwaskihk ta pêtâkosiw
kâya tâhkotahik
kâya mâtok
kâya wîhik

mistikwaskihk piko ta matwêwaw
thump-thump   *thump-thump*

kâya ta mîcêtwinânawiw
kâya ni ka wîhikawin
namôya kisipipayin

thump-thump   *thump-thump*

kâya iytatêyita atâmaskamik ta pimisinîyin
kâya ayimota kikway ta kî hikik
kâya pakicîtota mihtâtamowin

thump-thump   *thump-thump*

namôya iskwêyâni katamiskawin
niyaw piko pakicîmakan
kâya kîmohc pîkiskwê ka tipiskâk
namôya kiwanihin

thump-thump   *thump-thump*

ispîhk kanîtâwikîyan
kiskinohtahin, tâpiskohc nikâwiy otêh kêsi
pahkahokot nânâskomot
kâpê isi pimâtisiyan êkosi nikêsi ponâyitin

thump-thump   *thump-thump*

when I die

don't expect fancy
no stage to put me on
no crying faces

I only need the heartbeat of the drum
thump-thump   *thump-thump*

don't expect a crowd to gather
no mention of my name
no ending

thump-thump   *thump-thump*

don't expect to lie beneath the ground
don't talk of what might have been
no submission to sorrow

thump-thump   *thump-thump*

don't expect to say goodbye
only my body surrenders
no whispers in the night
no you have not lost me

thump-thump   *thump-thump*

guide me as my mother's heart
pulsing with gratitude
the day my life began
show me that I die as I have lived

thump-thump   *thump-thump*

namôya ayiwak, nikawî yêmikan, kikway
namôya nika pîkiskatên
namôya môsitân wîsakêyitamowin
nika pakicîtotên kâkikê pimatisiwin

thump-thump   *thump-thump*

nika nîmihiton

free of sadness
free of pain
free forever

thump-thump   *thump-thump*

I will dance

tapwêwin

tapwêwin
tânisisi kikway êyisi kakêtawê yitaman
    wîcêtômakanoh
    kiskisiwin
    kikway ê-wiyâpahtami

âtit ka wanikiskisin—âtit ka kiski nohamakon—âtit âcimôwina
—âtit wawêsîmakanoh
wiyâpahtamoki piyisk
âti kiskisinânawiw
piyisk âti pawâhcikâtêw

yikohk piko ê-kiskêyitamân
kakî wîhtamâtin
kîspin âyiwâk kikway
piko ta miskamâsoyin

tapwêwin

the truth
depends on perspective
    memory and imagination
    cannot survive
    without each other

some memories are lost—some are lessons—some are stories
—sometimes embellished

imagination powers memory
imagination builds dreams
a web spun in mind

the truth is—I can only tell what I know
    the rest
    you must find
    yourself

âcimowin

tâpiskohc wapakwanî
iskwêw wiyaw
akamâmakwak nimihitowak
âcimostawin

pikihtêw mâhkâpâtêw
nistam nikotwasik pipon
mâmowacêyask akîhtêwa
kistêyitakwanoh
âcimostawin

kôna pâhkisin
sîmikwasiw
wêwêkapiwak
wâsakam iskohtê
âcimostawin

story

a woman's body like a rose
blooming waist
butterflies dance
tell me a story

smoke expands
first six years
the most important
see
        hear
                touch
                        teach
journey beside
not ahead
tell me a story

snow tumbles
bearing the weight of sleep
draped in robes around fire
tell me a story

mîkiwahp

niyânanosâp apahswêya
kwayaskwaskisiw mîtos

hay hay

tâwâhi nistwâpitêwa
pîminakwan kikipâhta
âstisa takopicikâkêw wêstakaya

tâtakotasastaw kakêhtâwisiwina
kisikoh isi sowiniskêyow
pahkêkinwêsâkêw
otâcimowin wawêsîwâkêw
otêhi ohcipayiyow kâkîsimowin,
kitimâkêyimowin mîna pawâtamowin

iskwêwikamik
paskwâw mostoswayân
apâkwâkêw

hay hay

mîkiwahp

fifteen poles
straight-backed tree

thank you

three stand at middle
run roperunner run
sinew binds her hair

lay teaching upon teaching
spread her arms to the sky
enfold her in leathery skin
paint her gown with story
light her heart aflame
rise from her bosom
dream
love
pray

woman's lodge
family's home
sheltered by buffalo's back

thank you

ispayôwina

miskîsikwapoy
pahkitês tawapoy
pêyakwan isi nâkwanoh
awâsisak namôya nântaw itêyitamwak asiskîwapoy
nakatamâhko asikiy
kikîwêtotênaw asiskî
iskotêw mîna kitimâkêyitowin wîcêtomakanoh
kikîsôwinikonâw
yôtin kâkî kisiniyawêw apo miyo tâkiyawêw
pêyakwan ka paki tatâmoh

kitôwin namôya kotakawîyak pêhtam
kiya piko
kîkway namôya wîhkâhc ponâyitîmakan
kitacâhk

elements

I know that teardrop
is the same shape as rain

children don't mind the touch of mud—
we become earth in death

fire and love are the same
feeling of warmth to skin

wind can bite or refresh—
same as air pressed from a mouth

the voice that no one else can hear
        the part that is you
        the piece that never dies
is your spirit

âtayôkaniwiw kakayêsiwin

waskway mîtos
kikikapawiw ê-kîmasinâstêhokot
wîsâkêcâhkwa

tipahikêpayô kakayêsowin
âsô kâsispowîtâmâkan
êsi nihtâwiki pimâtisiwin

legends of betrayal

birch tree stands
with black strip scars
whipped by wesakechak

the price of betrayal
passed down in each
descending seed

moskwâpahcikêwin

napatêkâpî
âpihtaw askiy wâpâhta

pasakwâpi
patâpâhta wâsêw askîtakwâw
patâpim pîtosyiniw ê-pahpîwîkêyit
kâwâsâkonakâk

tôkâpi
môskêyihta anima askiy
anima nipiy
anima kîsik

wâpâhta askiy iyinîsiwin

perspective

close one eye
see the world in
halves

close both
miss the brilliance of blue
a kind stranger's smile
the shine of sun on snow

open both eyes
aware of the land
he water
the sky

observe the law of balance

miyo-ohpikinâwasowin

nipapakisâpahtên mîkiwâhp apaswêya kâ-tâpisinahami
miyo-ohpikinâwasowin

wanâmaw têpakohp ê-tâtoh piponêt—tanisi ê-itwêmaka?

mwêstas
nika-nisitohtên
          nêwosâp êkwa tâtoh piponêw
nikosis

miyo-ohpikinâwasowin

nitohta
naskota kâkakwê-cimikawiyin—
nêkâ tânêki?
nêkâ tânisîsi?

manâcih—
mâhtêsa nêkâ

kiskinohamaw nisîkahcê—
kitakohtânaw cî âsay?

nanâskomoh—
wâpahta kâ-osîhtamâtan nêkâ

kâkiyaw mîkiwahp kiski-nwahamâkêwina
mâmawacêyis kitimâkêyitowin

miyo-ohpikinâwasowin

I stare at the Tipi Teaching poster
good child-rearing

confusing for a seven-year-old—what does that mean?

much later
I would understand
       he's fourteen now—my son

good child-rearing

listen
answer questions—
mommy why?
mommy how?

be respectful—
excuse me mom

model patience—
are we there yet?

give gratitude—
look what I made you mom

all Tipi Teachings—but most of all
love

nikosis

nâpêkasow-iyiniw
namôya ospitoni mâka otêhi ohci
wicitaw otaskîkan
namôya kostam ta tâpwêt

nâpêkasow-iyiniw
namôya mahmicisiwakêw
mâka otacahkok ohci
nanâskomow awasisa ohci
manâcihêw wîcisâna
pêyâtikwê-yimototam
kâkiyâw kikway êspihtaskamikâ

nâpêkasow-iyiniw
namôya ohcîcihk ohci
wîcihêw kêhtêyaya
kiskinohtahêw oskâya
kicêyitam kîkwaya pêci nâway mîna
anohc êkê

nâpêkasow-iyiniw
namôya osâkowêwin
mâka onikamowin
kâkisimo ta-miyo kisikâyik
tâwihkôkâta pimâtisiwin
tawaspâwêhat yiyiniwacahkwa

my son

strength of warrior
is not in his arms
but in his heart
generosity of his hunt
care for community
courage to speak truth

strength of warrior
is not a physical feat
but in his spirit
thankfulness for children
respect for brother
composure to all creation

strength of warrior
is not in his spear
but in his outstretched hand
help for elders
guidance to youth
honor to harmony of past with present

strength of warrior
is not in his war cry
but in his song
prayer for a good day
celebration of life
awakening the spirit of a sleeping people

ipon

tipipêkan kayas-ayih
nôhkom omasinipayhon akotêyiw
namôya nohnakiskawâw

kîtâpasinaham kîkway
kânohtê otinikêt
kinîmihito-totam cîsâpêkahikan
âyispi tâkoskê-simô

kikiski-nohamawêw nikawiya têsi
paskososowêyit—kakanâcihit kinohsêwa—takisisamiyit mînisa

kinêso têhêw
oskanêwin kikisoskâko kisòkaniyiw okisêwâtisiwin
nikâwiy okiskisowina

kâkikê kî itwêw
kâpahpi kôtâkosik kiwî mâton
nisto-mitanaw askiya pwâmoyês nihtâwikiyan

nipasakwâpin ta-nipayân
êkôta ayâw

aspastâkan kikiskam
pahkwêsikana-pahkwênêsiw
ê-apiyit
kotawan-apiskohk

apiw nanahêkinam
kaskitêwâyiw mîna wapiskâyiw okîskasâkay
âpoh êtikwê askitakwâyiw—nîpâmâyataniyow—oskaskosiwâyiw
âstêtaw otoskwana

yvonne

clipped corners curve with age
a square snapshot hangs above the bed
the grandmother I never met

she drew pictures for words
on grocery lists
danced to fiddle
high step jig

she taught my mother
to cut hair—clean fish—cook berries

her heart was weak
rheumatic fever
her love was strong
mother's memories

she always said
giggles before dark end in tears
thirty years before I was born

I close my eyes to sleep
—this time she is here

she wears an apron
rips a piece of bannock
from the round
resting on the woodstove
she sits
flattens her black and white skirt
it could be blue—purple—green
rests her elbows

wêstakaya tâkoc tâkopitêyiwa
kâkikê yôcisin
wêscakasa itastaniywa wanawâhk
tâpiskoc masinipahiwini

kakikê kikikohtê nakiskâtin

itwêw
kikîpawâtitin nista mîna

her hair is tied on top
always with a breeze
kissing the wisps by her cheek
like the photograph

I always wanted to meet you

she says
I dreamed of you too

nitohta

nitohta
nôhkom nîkânokâpawiw
kinoyiwa osêkipatwâna
wapistikwanêsiw
tâpiskam otitimani mîna wasiskani
moscih osicikatêyiw nipâmayataniyiw okîskasâkay
opakwatêhoni isko wâkwani iskwayiw

nitohta
nôhkom pasow paskwâw-mostosiwikask
mîna maskosiwihkask
âpoh êtikwê namôya kîkway itêyitakwan mêkwahc
maka nitêhi ohci nikakiskisin
ka wikasko mâhkatêyiki
osêkêpatwana

nitohta
nôhkom mâci pîkiskwêw
wasiskani ohtêhi ohci pikiskwêw
nêhiyawêwin tipakotêw
kwâmwaci pîkiskwêw

nitohta
nôhkom itwê
nitohta

nitohta

nitohta
nohkom stands in front of me
her braids are long
edged with strands of silver
wrapping her neck—shoulders—breasts
her homemade skirt pours purple
from waist to ankle

nitohta
nohkom smells of sage
and sweetgrass—
it may mean nothing now
but my heart will remember
the scent of smudge
in her braids

nitohta
nohkom begins to speak
her words are formed
in her chest
—rolling nêhiyawêwin

gentle voice flooding the silence
nitohta—nohkom says—listen

$$\frac{niya}{Me}$$

namôya kîkway môyêtam

kâkî wîcêtin cî
ninîtahcowêpahtân kîcêkosîwnatikohk
    pakamîhtin iskwâtêm
nitatimâw nohtâwiy ati-pôsiw mihko owatowaswakanihk

opâhowipisim kisâstêw acisôw
iskwâtêm yohtênam pêkisâpâhtêpayôw
nisipwêpayinan mêskanahk

âcipicikan âcipitam êkwa nisîkac mâkoskawêw

misi-yotêkotêw wâsênaman—nipason asiskiy

nohtâwiy kwâmwatisiw anohc
mêskanâw wâwâkamon
wâkamon sisonê iykacawâsi

kitôcikan mêtawêmakan "misi-osawisiw tâkisî"
nisîkimâw nohtâwiy naskwahamâkê-mâka
piko ta-nakatôkêt mêskanaw

nitakopayinân—ni-nistawinên oma wâskahikan
kanakê pêyakwâw kapônâ pitakîsikak oma kâskîwik
nimêtawâkanan awâsisîkânak nihcâyihk mîna ê-kwaskôtiyak
ita kâkwâskohti

ninohtê kakwêcimaw nikâki pîhtiwan cî—maka nikânawâpamaw nohta
namôya—namôya katac takakwêcimak

mihtâtat cipahikanis mwêstas nohta pêwayawîw
sîtikwêyiw tânisi môsihiwiw namôya ninistawinên
oma kêsi nâkosit

nohta kîkway ôma êkî tasikama otênahk?
ê-nitawâpênawakik otênawiyiniwak—mâhti tanitahto

ignorant

"can I come with you?"
I run down the front steps
        slam through the screen door
                catch my dad getting into his red truck

hot august sun hits tanned skin
truck door opens a furnace—collected heat spills out on me
        we take off down the road

he shifts gears methodically—hand and foot moving in unison

my window wide open—gritty smell of gravel dust

my dad is quiet today—blank
        the road twists and
                    bends around sloughs

the radio plays "big yellow taxi"
—I coax my dad to sing—but
he needs to concentrate on the road

we pull up to a driveway—I know this house

at least one afternoon—every week this year
playing barbies in her basement
and jumping
on her trampoline

I want to ask if I can go in—but when I look at my dad
        no—I don't need to ask
ten minutes later my dad comes out
mouth a tight line—eyes holding some emotion
        I don't know this look

kêpê itisawâcik otawasimisiwawa askikanihk kiskinohamatowin
awiyak cî niwîcêwâkanak
namôya
       tânêki?

nohtâwiy piko tanâkatokêt mêskanaw—
nikinâ
nimiskawâw nikâwiy
tânisi oma ê-itwêmaka namôya kîkway môyêtam?

"dad, what were we doing in town?"
"surveying the town people—how many will send their kids to our band school."
"any of my friends?"
"no"

       "how come?"
my dad needs to concentrate on the road—
at home

      I find my mom

         "what does ignorant mean?"

nitawi kiskêyita

nohtâwiy wâpâstêwtâsêw pêyâkwâw kîci mihtâtâtomtanaw
kêkâmihtayatwaw mihtâtâtomtanaw nikotwâsomtanaw
sênapânêkin pakôwayân osâwi atoskêw astisa
câpiskâkanêkinos paskwêpisiw

nitânis pâpascôpiw pîsikistikânihk namôya nâkatôkêw ohi nâpêwa
kâsamaskapiyit
asiskiy ê-mâmitonêyitamîyit

apwêsiyiwa

âstam nôsim

nitânis sisonê wîcêkô nohtâwiy mâmaskâtêw asiskiw môhtêwa

discovery

my dad in faded denim—a 1960s hockey jersey—yellow work
gloves—kerchief tied over brow

nitânis skips through rows of flowering peas—oblivious to the
meditations of a man hunched over black dirt

sweat mixing with soil

âstam nôsim!

nitânis by his side—my father caught in the curiosity of an earth-
worm's mysteries

takwahiminâna

nikî mawosonân mâna takwahiminâna awaswâhi sakâsi nikinâ
ôhci opahowipîsim kâtahkotâkosik, askikosak tâkopisiwâk nipak-
wâtêhonahk nisocîcîya nimawiswâkânân mâmatwêtinwa mînisa
askîkosi niwîyapahtênan minisâpoy tasîkinama nohtâwiy kîsiswâci
napaki pahkwêsikana ayamihêwkîsikâki

anohc nitawâsimisâk namôya kakî mawosôwâk anihi takwa-
himinâna kakanawâpahtênaw ê-piscipohtâcik itâmi askiy ispayiw,
ocêpîkosa mîna minisatikohk piscipôtâwak kawîsakan mînisapoy

kipikwanêwêtâwak mînisa

chokecherries

we used to pick the chokecherries around the bend of bush behind
our house—cool august nights—pails belted to our waists—two
hands pulling berries between curled fingers—

the constant patter against the plastic pail brought dreams of syrup
drenching dad's sunday pancakes

now—my children can't pick those chokecherries—we can only sit
and watch pesticide poison cloud the bush—rain down on leaves—
imagine the pungent sting as it seeps into soil—runs the roots—
swims up sap streams—stealing the lovely taste of our sunday syrup

choking berries

okiskinohamâkêw omasinahikêwinisa

nâpêsisâk têpakohposâp itâtohponêw âpô cî ayi ayinanêwosap âpô
nîstanaw ayiwâk pêyak nikotwâw êkoni âpô cî kâhkiyaw

nohcihitowipîsim 2006
pêpihtokwêw ita kakiskinohamâkeyan anohc pahpi wîkwêyiw
takâkwê kâtât omôsihowin

yiyikopêwpîsim 2006
takî-yikin pîtos têsikaskimak—ninêstwêyitên "âpo-êtikwê" tâhtwaw
kîkway kâkakwêcimak—tanisi kâkî isi sâpôcimak?

kaskatinow-pîsim 2007
âsamina nêstosiw itwêw misi têtapiwinihk êki nipat ohtâwiya
wîkiyihk tanihêwa okâwiya?

yiyikopêwpîsim 2007
pêyak ayamihêw kîsikâw tatêpipayiyan nimîkawin minisîkâna
niwayawîn kapê wayiniyân wâkas pihtonikan astêw wêpinikêwinihk
pêyak kîsikâw piko têpipayinohminisîkana osam iskwêsisapoy
ayiwâk itêyitâkwaniyiw wiki yiyoh pahkwêsikana

ayîkipîsim 2008
namôya nikîsîtânan otatoskêwin kâkikê nêstosiw soniyawas-
inahikan kîsikâw astêmâhcihow ohtawakaya namôya êka tapêhta
pitikoniskêyiwin mohtêyapiskwa pastitinoh kîkâtowin kâkwêskisin
misitêtapiwinihk kiyâm tanipâw

pawâcakinâsîs 2008
pipon kêcinac êkwa namôya oskotâkâw ohtâwiya atâwêyiwa pêyak
mistikowat iskwêsisapoy nimiyaw niskotâkay nitâkwaskitinik
êkwêyac pâhpîwîkwêyêw

teacher notes

boys—17 years old—maybe 18 or 21
it's one of them and all of them

September 2006
he walked into my classroom today—hiding behind a smirk

November 2006
I'm tired of blanket "whatevers" for every question I ask—how do I
get through the walls he has up?

October 2007
he's tired again—he said he slept on his father's couch—where is his
mother?

November 2007
the school gives me a bowl of fruit once per week—I left the room
for a while today—when I came back banana peels were draping
the garbage can—my bowl empty—because beer is more important
than bread at home

April 2008
he's always tired on cheque day—we didn't get through the math
lesson—he said he tossed on the couch all night—fists crashing—
bottles breaking—voices yelling—I let him sleep

December 2008
winter is definitely here now—he still doesn't have a jacket—his dad
bought a case instead—so I gave him one—he gave me a hug—it's
the first time he smiled at me

kisêpîsim 2009
nimetawânân pahkâtowan asôwata namôya yîtasi mâmitonêyitam
ocîhciya ohci kiskêyitam tatôta makâyis êkosi êtikwê êpêyisi
waskawîtota kâhkiyaw kîkway

ayîkipîsim 2010
kisipipayin kîsikâw nitêpwâtaw kanawêyimiso kinohtê wâpamitin
wâpahki niwastahamak pâpîkiskwêw êkwa ayimihcikêw
masinahikêw pâhkatowêw kêyapich nânipaw soniyawasinahikan
kîsikâw âskaw kitowêkwâmo nititêyimaw âskaw êpawâta

paskâwêhow pîsim 2010
âsôhotêw anohc nimoskwêyitên kwêskâyitiniyiw otaskî mîna nista

February 2009
we played basketball—it's uncanny the way his hands know what
to do with the ball—react—don't think—but I guess he's had to do
that in a lot of situations

April 2010
at the end of the day I called to him—be safe—I want to see you
tomorrow—he waved back—he talks in class now—reads—writes
—plays basketball—he still sleeps after cheque day—sometimes he
snores—when he awakes he tells me his dreams

June 2010
he walked across the stage today—I cried—the world has changed
for him—for me too

ayiwâk tipahikan pîsimwân

wantipiskastêw
pisisikwastêwa atoskêw têtapiwina
      oskaskosiw mînisîkan iskosâwatêwa
      iskwascikan

swoosh swoosh
okanâcîcikêw owêpahikan kitowêtatâw

pâhkisimôwin masinipayiw nakwan
wâsênamâwini ohci

nicihcîsa pahpatinikêmakwanoh
      kitowêtinoh âpikwahikana

okâwimâw moskâtêyitam

apiscîtâkwân—cipahikanis atitam
tipahikan miyâskamôpayiw

mâmitonêhicikan kisiskâpayiw
      kiskêyitamâwin kikî kiskinohamâkân
      namôya kitêpitôtên kîkwaya
      konta kiyakapiwin
namôya ki naskomikon

overtime

dark hallways
empty desks
      cucumber slices
      half-eaten dinner

swoosh swoosh
the janitor's broom

sunset framed
by window panes

fingertips fumble
      tapping keys

guilty mother's conscience
mall sound—secondhand as it catches
time passing

thoughts steamroll
      lessons taught
      unmet objectives
      nonsense giggles
no answers

apohêtikwê

kî yotin
âpohcî kimôwan papakamihtin wâsênamawini
mâka tâpiskohc mîki ê-ispakosit

kisisiwâk kokosimihko wîkikasosak tâhkapiwâk

kî kisitêw
apohcî kôna pâhpakiyita akocin maskosîhk
mâka tâpiskohc nikamon itîtâkosiw

niyoskitên kitohcikan

kî tipiskâw
apohcî kîsikâw pîsim sâkastênam
mâka tâpiskohc êkîsônit

pakâpôwayan kîsonam yiyikisicanisa kâ pipo

maybe

it was windy
or maybe the rain was rapping against the window
but he smelled like home

hot chocolate chip cookies cooling on the counter

it was hot
or maybe the snow was hanging in patches on the grass
but he sounded like a song

a soft piano melody stroking my ears

it was dark
or maybe the sun was lighting the room
but he felt like comfort

soft flannel sheets warming cold toes in winter

nipâwin niwîmaskakon

kâ kwâmwata kâkiyaw kîkway kisîwêw
konita kikwaya nimêskwapahtên
mâsîtâmakanoh takî kwâmwacayayân

pîkwêyitamôwina
kipawêyitên kâ wâpah
têpwêmakanoh
         ka pasakwâpiyan

sleep evades me

the silence makes everything
louder
looming emergencies break through
wrestling with   the quiet I deserve

worries
brushed off in daylight
become sirens
            when I close my eyes

têpiya pîkiskwêwina

macîhtwâwin
nicîpotônêyin
tâpiskohc sîwinikan mîna wîsakosâwas ispakwan

kîmohc pîkiskwê
namôya kipêhtawâw ê-itwêt
ayisiniskêyiw
nititwahok
namôya mîwacisiw
pasci mamitonêyita kîkway takî îki mêkwahc
namôya kwayaskopayiw
kamiyito

tâpiskohc kimôwanâyâw
pîkiskwêwin kâpahkitêk
nitônihk
pâpahkawin
yîkwaskwan pîhkwêyitamômakan
namôya awiyak mîwêyitam kimôwan
niya piko

namôya kwamwahc ayâmakan
tâpiskohc niya
âspîs niwâpamikawin âspîs nipêhtakawin
âspîs ninisitohtâkawin
kâkêkâhc nipômân
mâka nisôkêyitên

mâmitonêyita
kocista
pîkiskwê
masinahikê
têpiya pîkiskwêwina

just words

cantankerous
I purse my lips
the taste both sugar and lemon

whisper
inaudible slurs
met with gestures
pointing at me
bitter
overthought moments
of indiscretion
shared

precipitation
the word that pops
on my lips
the drip-drip serenade
grey clouds are depressing
nobody likes rain
except me

teetering
like me
rarely seen, heard, understood
nearly toppling
but holding ground

think
taste
speak
write
just words

mâtwân cî ôma

tanêki wâsaskotêw manicôs kâ wâsisot
tanêki êkâ kâsapwâsoyân

tanêki—mwêstas pêyak wâsaskotêwmancôs—kotak cî wâsaskotê-
payiw
ê-ohtêyitocik cî tanakatokâtîcik
êmawonêtocik cî
âpho cî êwasaskotê-namâtocik tamiskâtocik katipiskâyik

tânisîsi kêyisi miskâkawîyân tipiskâ

kâkî waspâwê-askitêw cî nihtêhi
        (nôhkom nikî wîhtamâk 'iskotêw' kânêhiyawê iskwêw ohtêhi
        itwêmakan)

kîspin nitiskwêwin iskotêwin cî nihtêhi

(kâya mêtawâkê iskotêw nôhkom kî-itwêw)
                mâtwân cî itwêmakan kâya mêtawâkê iskwêw ohtêhi

kîko mêtawêwin kâ-mêtawêcik
kâkî astawêyapawêw cî iskotêw
tâniwê niwâsisowin

mâtwân cî ôma

why does firefly glow?
why can't I be translucent?

why—after one firefly—does another one light up?
do they envy for attention? is their luster a competition? do they simply
shine to find one another in the night?

how will I be found in the dark?

if a spark can restart my heart—is it conceivable to say there is fire inside
me?
    nôhkom taught me 'fire' in Cree translates to 'woman's heart'

if I am woman my heart must be flame—right?

don't play with fire warned nôhkom
    does this mean don't play with woman's heart?

what is this game they play?
can it drown all light from burning embers?
where is my glow?

nipâw

niyâyinamwân omaskinâskisowin A
nâspici kamasinâsot
itâmi wasakâ
ohtêhi pâhkahokô
nipêhtâwân onipâwin tapêhtamwâk
ocîcî watâ astêyiw
tâwâhi âkôpicikanêkinoh pêwasistêw
ninâkatokân ê-pahpîwîkwêyit
otônihk
ita kâkî ocêmâk

he sleeps

sliding my finger over the A
his tattoo—ink etched forever
below his skin

his heart ticks away
seconds of sleep in my ear

caught in the intersection
between chest and shoulder
his hand rests on bare waist

light parts the curtains
I notice the smile
on lips I have kissed

nisto pîkiskwêwina wîcihitômakanwa

nistam pakitatâmôwin
    mihkoyawêw
    ê-isi pâhkahiko isi siswêpayin mihko
mâcî kîsôsonânawiw
kâsiskani isko misiwê

êkwa mâmitonêhicikan
tâpôwakêyitâ-mômakan
iskwêyâni

the effect of three words

first breath
      the blush of pink on oxygen-starved skin
      blood pulsing—warmth spreading
outward
chest to limbs

and the mind believes
last

aspin wiyê iskwêyani

anima kêtîtâkosiyan
    tâpiskohc kâ-pêmihkwaskwa
kasîmihkwasi nâkosi
    tapiskohc sîwapoy ê-sîkinamih êta
    ê-ayêcisi masakâ
konita kâpahpîkaso
    kanawâpahta nipiy ê-âsiciwa
    nanawâ
ê yisi kanawâpamiyan
    nômaskatin
    tâpakitêyitami aspin wiyê
anima kîsikâw sipwêtêyin

the last time

the color of your voice—scarlet
    piercing like dawn
    on sleep-hungry eyes
the scent of speech—sharp like vinegar
    stinging open wounds
    on naked flesh
the comfort of laughter—a mocking smirk
    watching water cut paths
    down my cheek
the touch of your gaze—frostbite
    engulfing the past
the day you left

kâya kimiyosin isin

namôya kiwâpahtên wînan
pîcâyi ôta niskîsikohk—itâpi itâm
itê sêkisiwin êmicini-kêmaka masinahikêwina
kiyaskiwina kâpê pêhtamân
namôya nitâpatakêyimâw nâpêw tapêhtawâk—pisisikwâyiw
opîkiskwêwin
nipê-mâton—nipê kiyaskin—nipê-nîpêwisin
takiskinohamân nipacî-nikêwina
ni mâmacisostâkon—namôya nôhtê sipwêtêmakanoh

siswêtêmakan nimâmtonêyicikan wantipiskâ kânipâyân
itê êpêhot
ocîcîya ôhci mâci âyinam niyaw
kâsâminit niwânêyimon
êkôta kisâcîmakan
kaskaskitênam—nimanâcihisowin
nikîmo-twatêmon

namôya kiwâpahtên âhkwan—nikipikwanêwênikon
niwîhowina—wînih—mâyâtis—kiskânak nikitimâkimik
nipê mâton—nikiyâskin - osâm ninêpêwisin
nikostâci-kwastimikon
wêsâmih namôya kwayask nikîmosihon kîhtwam

namôya kiwâpahtên kâ wîna
masinastêwa micîciya—ita pakwâtamôwin masinahikêpayin
nikîskwêyêtamik wanih-itwêtaw wiyâtikosiwin
iyâhkîtap kiskêyitam nêpêwataham

ninîmîstên kisiwâsiwin
nipê nôtinên—anihi kiskisôwina—kostêyitâkwan
êyisi-pêwêpisiyan

don't call me beautiful

you don't see the mess
inside these honest eyes—look deeper
where fear holds the debts
of tangled lies I've heard
      I despise the sound of a man—empty words
I've been crying—lying—too shy
to explain—the mistakes
too haunting—not wanting
to leave

my mind scatters to dark pockets of slumber—where he waits
from the moment he traced my body with his fingers
      writing his touch into my unconsciousness
where it lingers—
ashes from charred years—smearing my dignity
in muffled tears

you don't see the pain—strangling grip choking
my names—dirty—ugly—stupid bitch
his lips ruin me with words
I've been crying—lying—too shy
to explain
buried under nightmares
too real—to feel normal again

you don't see the mess
      these scarred hands—where hate is the debt
neurotic insults interrupt happiness
        in a hypnotic thumping of shame
I dance to anger

I've been fighting—inviting the memories in—frightful—insightful
to who I have been

namôya ki-wâpahtên kâ-wîna
âyîci kiyâskîwin—astawêna mihtâtamowin
nikakwê kâsôn—nitânwêtên—nitêpwân
namôya kihtwâm nika sâkôcihikawin

kiyâskis wihta kitâcimôwina
mâka kâya kimiyosin isin

you don't see the mess
below guarded lies—smothered with regrets
I try to hide—doubting—shouting
    I will never fall again

liar—tell your stories
but don't call me beautiful

nicawâsimis

ni wahpâtên ka-nêpêwisiyin
maka namôya kâkî-kâsiyâpawahaw kasakay

âpoh êtikwê namôya kinisitohtên
tâpasinah kitâcahk kimâmitonêhicikan ohci

âpihkon sênapan - pîhtona wêwêkâpicikan
mîkowisiwin ôma kiya

my child

I see your shame
but color will not wash from your skin

maybe you don't understand
trace your spirit with your thoughts

untie the bow—peel the wrapping
you are a gift

pîkwêyitamowin mâyimâcihowin

nêstwacâpiwina kiwâpahtên wâpamonihk
piyêsîs pêyakwâw kâkî pimihat—pâkisin
kipêyitamisin
namôya kîhêhêw mâmâhkatâmow

êyîwahapit nitawi kiskisiw
pâhpiw yotin—âyîtinam yikwaskwanwa

nêstwêyitam wêpinakêyitam takîsêyitamâsot
misikinosêw wâpahtam kawêcitat—tamîcisot
nohtê pakicîtotam kawêpihikot sâkocihikô
kwêskwê tipahkocin—kiskwêsin
mâci makwêyimo—iskwatâmo
otâtam êkâ tapêtaht

ê-atipasakwâpit kiskisiw
soskwâpoyiw wiyâtokôcowani
tâkipayiw timihk

wiyaw sâkocihikow
kisiwêw mîcêtinânihk
ospitona—oskâta—ostikwân
kotâwiw
tâpiskohc miskinahk
kâkimôtapiw
kâsostam kostânisiwina
âkônam
kanâwêyitam opêyakowin

ê-âti pasakwâpit mâkwêyimow
kôstam
sêkisiw
sêkisiw

anxiety disorder

tired eyes look in the mirror
     where the bird once flew—it has fallen
     air crushing chest
     breathless shoulders panting

dimming eyes reminisce
     laughing winds—embracing clouds
     circling—swooping—rising

exhausted mind depresses reason
     the sturgeon sees an easy meal
     submitting to temptation—hooked
     flopping—flipping
     out of its element
     instinct raises panic—mouth gasps
     drowns in such openness

dimming eyes remember
     sliding through current
     cooling in the depths

devastated body out of control
     in a loud—crowded room
     turtle's arms—legs—head
     withdraw into the dark shell
     peering out at a world of unknowns
     submerged in terror—barricaded
     protected solitude

dimming eyes cower
     in fear
     fear
     fear

wâhkôtowin

misi-otênak toronto wêsâmi-asiniskâw
nikôtawêyimâwak acâkosak—mîna kâ-pahkisimok
ninohtêkatân—nohtâwiy itwêw nête mîciwin astêw
itwaham ê-osâwâsaskitêk mîcisôkamik
nititâpin
     namôya awiyak niki-tâpamik
     namôya awiyak kiskêyitam niwîhowin
êkôta kâ-wâpamak

askito-tâsêw—tomistikwânêw—wîhkwâkan yisinâkwaniyiw
namakîkway êmôyêta
tâpiskohc ohi kâ-wantipiskastêki wâsênamâna ispiwâskahikana
kâwasakaskâkoyan
nikanawâpamâw ê-nahastâsot
ita sôniyâw kâ-otinit—yiyikopêw-pîsim kisin-tipiskâw

nohtâwiy pêhosiw iskwahtêmihk—itê-êyitâpiyan itâpiw

nikanâwâpamik
ê-tâkopitaman nimaskisin
kâkî tôpicikêwak sêkêpahisak
iskwêw wahkwaskisiyan matwêtinoh
nipêhtên
tanisi tântê ohci kiya

ninawakîn nitâkopitên nimaskisn
nohtâwiy kâwihitohtêw ita sôniyaw kôtinit
kitôpicikêwak sêkêpayisak—iskwêw-askisina matwêtinoh
âta êkisîwêk nipêhtawâw nohtâwiy tanisi tanitê ohci kiya?

wâhkôtowin

on the streets of toronto—overwhelmed by concrete
      I miss the stars—the sunset at home

I'm hungry—dad says there's food on yonge
pointing at the yellow neon sign—diner

I look up the street
      nobody makes eye contact
      nobody knows my name
then I see him

grey sweatpants—oily hair—his face wears a look
more empty
than the dark windows of the skyscrapers
that surround me

I watch him make a bed
beneath the ATM—november nights are cold

dad pauses at the door—follows my gaze

I bend to tie my shoe—dad walks back to the ATM
      car horns blare past—a woman's heels clip clop
amidst the noise I hear dad—tansi where are you from?

niwâpamâwak niso nâpêwak sakicicêntowak acimostâtowâk
nohtâwiy miyêw katêpinêhamiyit mîciwin
mêkwâ asiniskâ niwâpahten
namôya wâhyaw niwîkin—toronto misi-iskonikan ota kanâta

wêsâmi yoskâwa napacâkosa
nohtâwiy nitik kâkikê kitêpipayinaw ta-miyâya kîcisâninaw

I witness two men shake hands—share a story—dad passes him
enough for a meal
in the midst of the concrete—I see
I am not that far from home—toronto—the biggest reserve in
kanata

and over soggy french fries
dad tells me—we always have enough to give to our brothers

yînto pahkwêsikan tipiskâwa

mihko nâskana
osâwihtakâw
namôya nikî nipân

nitasawâpin
wâsênâkwan wâsakâm iskwâhtêmi
kîmohc nipimi-tâcimon
êkâ tamisihoyân

namôya nimôsihikawin
nikanawâpamâw nohtâwiy
sîkinam
       itêwêw
             mâmâkonêw

nikiskino-wâpin
têsi pahkwêsikanî-kêyân

bannock nights

my eyes wander
     red plush carpets
     yellow vinyl floors
sleepless nights

light beckons around door hinges
I crawl quietly
to avoid punishment

unnoticed spectator—I watch my father
pour
     stir
          knead

my hands learn the rules
of making bannock

nikâwiy opîkiskwêwin

awastipiskohk nikî-kimotin kino-tâpân
iskotêw-apoy kîsiwâw
nikawacin nisita
niposiwê-pinikwâk sêkêpayisi
namôya wasaskotawêw
têpiya tispiskâw
yiyikawân
wâwâkamon mêskanâw

sakâ
kipêhtâtin

mohtê-âpiskwa sêwêhtinoh
nîpin
kaskapahtêw nipason
nitayônisi
nitôni
macipakwa wihkimastêw
mâka namôya nikiskisin
mwêstas tanisîsi ê-yispayik

kîkisêpa
kipêhtâtin

nisâposciwêpinik wâpamonâpiskohk
nitoskwan nimôsîtân
nîcikwan nikâskihtân
pisisikwâw wâskahïkan
pisisikwâw nipêwin
nipakitina mâtonân

nakîhtakohk
kipêhtâtin

my mother's voice

I stole a van the other night
whiskey tasted warm—my feet were cold

they shoved me in the car
no headlights—just darkness—fog folding over the hood
curling backroads

in the trees
I heard your voice

bottles clinked
summer—tangy bonfire scent
on my clothes

in my mouth—weed tasted sweet—but I don't remember
what happened after

in the morning
I heard your voice

he pushed me through the window
my elbow stung—scraped my knee

empty house—empty bed
we made love

in the walls
I heard your voice

miskîsik-wâpoy namôya nôkwan yiyikâw-asiskiy
sâpopêw kâkî-kimôwa
nimâmasinahên
kîkway piko kâtipiyawêhoyân
niwîhowin
tanikota kê-ayâyin
nititwân
kikî tâpwân
takî pôyoyân

tears don't show on sand wet from rain
I drew loops with fingers
traced my only possession—my name

wished you were there—I'd say
you were right

I should have stopped

pimicâyi nipimâpin

nikotwâsik miscîcân kispakisiw miskwamiy
mâci pîwan
namôya sêkisiw
kanawâpâhtamwan ocîciya
kiso pâhkêkinwêcisêw
kêkahc ayikiskawêw wasakaya
awâsisak kwâmwacisiwak nâway

nikân ôtatwâ
misi-âwatwâwaswakan pêpatâpôyow
kêkâhc nimisiwêpayitân nitêyaniy
ninakînân

niso tipahipîsimwân nitapin
nipêhon
nikanawapamâw kona ê-ispapit
ninohtê ayêciskin konihk
ita namôya kîkway ê-nokwa
nikwâ-mwâcisin

riding shotgun on the coquihalla

six inches of ice
blizzard rage
no panic attack
watching her hands
soft padded fingers
glued to leather
knuckles nearly piercing skin
kids quiet in back

in front of us
semi slides to the ditch
I nearly swallow my tongue
we stop

two hours I sit
waiting on coquihalla
gazing at fortress snowbanks
wanting to make a footprint
on unexplored kingdoms
secure in silence

âniski-ohtâwîmâw

kaskitêwaw mîna wâpiskaw ki wâpamitin
êyisîhoyin askito-nâkwanoh

âpîhtaw
wâpistowêw
mikotawêwaniskwêw
pêyak âyônis kikiskam
mâkititimanêw
osîkikwêw
pîkwêyitam-nâkosiw
wipasinâsiw capasis oskîsikoh

kicîciya peyakwan tapiskohc nohtâwiy
sôkanoh
atoskê-winakwanoh

nanêtaw sasitosiw
apisis wâkâwkanêw
kaskitêw-tâsêw
kêyapihc ki pâhkêkinêskisinân
wihtamawin tânitê ê-ociyan

great grandfather

in black and white
I see you as a blend of greys

mixed blood
ashy colored beard—wavy hair
charcoal starchy suit—broad shoulders
furrowed brow—deep pockets of stress
under your eyes
darker than the rest of your face

your hands look like my father's
strong and big—open
made for work

an uncomfortable stiffness
your posture slumped a bit
posed in black cotton pants
still—moccasins you wear
tell me where I come from

mâhkacâp

kôcâwîsinâw kikî yisihikâtik mâhkacâp
mâhkacâp

nisîmis
nisîmis

kisâkihitin
kisâkihitin

mâhkacâp
ê-yisi mâhkacâpiyin
ki-wâpamin

mâhkacâp

uncle called you mâhkacâp
     big eyes

nisîmis—my little sister
kisâkihitin
I love you

mâhkacâp
with your big eyes
you see me

nistês

nistês
ki tâkahkitên
nitayisinên
ê-iysi waskawiyin—êyisînîkêyin
nitayisinên ê-iysi konita ê-itwêkâsoyin
kitaskôtin
asiniya kitâkiskâwâwâk
kiwîsakistêsinin

kiya nîkân kikî-sipwêtân
namôya kôhaskotin
ayikin
wâyow ocih osâm

kikwâ mwâtisin
êkosi piko nîsta
takwâ-mwatisiyan

my big brother

nistês
flattered you
mimicked your
moves—your style
catch-phrase jargon
followed you
kicked rocks that
hurt your feet

you left first
   I could not follow
time has a way
of creating distance

you sent silence
   I could only return
silence

nitânis

kitawasimisak pêhowak tanîtâwikicik
nitohta kitêhi
mosîtâ mocikisiwin
kiskêyita pîkiskâtisiwin
nitohta kimamitonêyicikan

tânisi êyis apit
êyis pîkiskwêt
nanâskomowin nohkôtaw
kitimâkeyimowêw
yiyospisîw cîcêw
tâpwêwin pîkiskwâtam

manâcihiso ê-iskwêwiyin
otê nîkâni okâwîmaw

my daughter

your children waiting to be born
hear your heart
feel your excitement
know your sadness
listen to your thoughts

dignity in a woman
the way she sits
tone of her voice
gratitude she presents
love she shares
gentleness of her hands
honesty she speaks

respect yourself as a woman
mother of tomorrow

kisê-pîsim pimâsow

kônisak kona
tâpiskohc êwanâsit
cikâscêpayisi
ka awasisîwih

nitawasimisak
tâpiskohc nistêsak
kâkî-kihtocik
kiskinohamâ-tôkamikohk

micîciya
tâpiskohc nikâwiy
kâsasîhtêyita mâna kâpapêciya
niyânan-cipahikanis
kâhkiyaw kîkway ôhci

miskwamiy
tâpiskohc ka-patinikêyân
pokwîspi
kâkikê

january drive

snowflakes—like stars at warp speed
on the tv at home
in childhood

my kids—like my brothers
pushing and pulling opinions
in high school

hands—like my mom
tense when we were five minutes late
for anything

ice—like I'm going to lose control
any minute
all the time

âcimowak

nisis micisonâtikoh sonêpiw
italy itwêw
êkotê kâkî nakata ocîcîs
notinikêw askiy
takotani namôya omamitonêhicikan wanîtât
pahpîwikwêyiw

nisikos
pâhkwaham ocîciya
nahêkinam pâkwayâkanan
sikinam maskikiwapoy

nikâwiy itêham ominikwâcikan
kwâ mwâtan
têpiya kipêhtên nôhkom ominikwâcikana
ê-sêwêtahamih

nohtâwiy pâhkwênêsiw wîkîkasosa
otêyani apisîs ahêw
namôya mâmâkwamêw
kôkosimihko wâwîkistam

nitawi wîcimêtawêm awâsisak
namôya kikway nohtê pahtinam

nisis nânâmiskwêyêw
kîhtwam mâci âcimow

stories

uncle sits at the table
        italy—he says
that's where he left his finger
        battlefields
lucky he didn't lose his mind
he chuckles

auntie checks the kettle
wipes her dry hands—folds a dishtowel in a tight rectangle—pours
the tea

mom stirs her cup
        quiet
except for the clink of metal
on kokom's shiny white china

dad breaks his cookie
places a piece on his tongue—doesn't chew
savoring the taste of chocolate

"go and play with the kids"
"she doesn't want to miss anything"

uncle nods—begins his story again

nohtikwêw

nohtikwêwow
âhâsô wâhkomowêw
itê êwikit

maskawasakêw
êtotakot pipon-yawêwon
atoskêwin kâ-nîpiniyik

ocîciya
manâhô maskîkiya
mawosô
mâmataham pâhkêkin

sinikonam ita kâkâkîcisit
tomihkwêw
sêsawinam oskana

niwihtamâk
ê-tâtâkômowêt
awasimê ita êwikit
ê-nohtikwêt

nohtikwêw

she is old
her family extends
beyond her home

tough skin
weathered by winter
worked in summer

her hands
gathered teas
picked berries
scraped hide

rubbing away pain
polishing wrinkles
massaging brittle bones

she tells me
her family extends
beyond her home
ê-nohtikwêt

kiskisiwin pawâtamowin

pêcinâway wâpakwaniya konowisinoh

                          âkwacisinoh

otakawâso pêho ê-kisintâkosik
tasakicicênât
tâkwaskitinât
nakiskawêw
itê kitocikêwin êkisîwêk
ayisiyiniwâk nêstosiwak
wanwêwtamwak mîna wanatakwan
pahkahoko wâskiskani
ita êkanawêyita owîhoniyow

kikisêpâ kîmohc piskiskwêwin nitawi kiskisi pawâtamowina

                          atiwanihomakanoh êsîmikwasi

wîkwâkan sîmihkwaso-nakwaniyo
pêkopayiw êkanawâpamikot
kanawâpamêw ê-postayonisêyit
kaskitêw masinâskisow wasaka
konisa oskâtikohk okwayâ
micîciya otitinamoyow omâmitonêyicikan
pakitâkiyawêtotam
pisikwâtêyitam tanikê-êsa
namôya kisipipayik

memory or dream?

flowers from the past—rose petals tipped with snow

                                                             delicately frozen

a lover waits in evening chill
to hold her in his palm
draw her under his arm
she meets him
where music crowds the streets
people leaning on tired hips
circle musicians
choruses of laughter drowning in the beat
drums in his chest
where her name is safe

morning whispers—reminiscent of dreams

                                                        fading in sleepy eyes

trace the curves of his face
he wakes to her gaze
sees her dressed
only in black ink and skin
snowflake kisses on forehead—neck
fingertips capture her thoughts
serenading her body to dance
passion—desire—wishing
it would not end

nohtâwiy oskîsikwa

wâsêkamin sâkahikanis
osâwa-sakêw
askitako pakowayân
kika-nâkwaniyîwa oskîsikwa

môhci itâpow
ê-nîtawapihitoyit
tâpiskohc êpakwatitocik

kâwiya tawâsêkam-atawâpiwak
nitâwasimisak
isi kâkisimo

my father's eyes

cerulean pools
bronze skin
turquoise shirt
brings out his eyes

looking to the floor
hearing the taunts of schoolchildren
hatred lacing their chants

do not let my children's eyes be blue
a quiet prayer

tohtosâpopîmî nikikinên amômay

ninohtê wayawîstamâson—namôya êkâ tanâkatôkêyan
wâpamonihk nêhpê-mamôyiwa ospikêkana—tâpiskohc êskana
otikwana isi nakwaniyiwa
ê-kisîpêkit miyomâhcihow—kisâkamitêwapoy otîtimani tâtêyitamihiko
nohtê pwâkomo ênohtêkatêt

namôya wîcihik maskîkiwiyiniwa

tohtohsâpopîmî kiki-amômay kikisêpa mîciw
       têpiya tapimatisit
       môya kîkway pîtos ki-otinam
âsônê kîkisêpâ—kisiskâ pâhkahokô
       kêyapic tipiskâw wayawîtimihk
       wâsaskotênikêw
nokohêw minahikosa kitimâkinakosiw
apisîs piko akocikanêwina
kêkahc pisikosiwâk asikanak

pêyak pisisikwaw soniyaw-kamik masinahikan

simîkwasiyiwa otawâsimisa—mitoni kîkway yiyitêtamîyiwa
ati sîtâskikanê mâhcihow
namôya hêhêw—wîwanêyitam—akamâmakosak—kisitêyiw ohkwâkan
tâhkicîcêw
otêhi pâhkahokow kitowê-tawakêw
namôya kâya mêkwâhc
kîskimi-kâtêw

butter mixed with honey

the urge to pee is bearable—but impossible to ignore
in the mirror her ribcage juts—hipbones stick like antlers from her waist
the shower feels good—hot water eases tension in shoulders
nauseated—her empty stomach flutters

doctors are no help

butter mixed with honey for breakfast
enough to keep her alive
all her stomach will tolerate
mornings always the worst—adrenaline rushes pulse
still dark outside—she turns on the lights
showing the pitiful two-foot christmas tree
the tiny pile of presents
near-empty stockings

one empty bank account

sleep-crusted eyes of her children—anxious looks of expectation
anxiety creeps into her chest

no breath—faint head—butterflies—hot flushed face
cold hands
heart pounding amplifies in her ears
no, not now!
legs go numb

nimîhtatên ôtênamok akotamâkowina—okâwimaw piko ta-pimisi
môya-ana mistahi wayiskam anâskân—pasakwâpô
kwaskwê-wêpinam aspiskwêsimon
iyiko ê-pômêt
wîcihin

kîmohc itwêw ispimîtakohk
mosîtaw kihtwâm nohtê-wayawîstamasow

"sorry—open your presents—mom has to go lie down"
the mattress barely dents—she closes her eyes
throws a pillow soaked
with disappointment

"help"

a whisper to the ceiling
and the urge to pee again

kâ-wâpamiyin niya

kiwâpamâw cî iskwêsis ê-pimohtêt
ê-wîcêwat omosôma
yoski nêhiyaw kâkîsimowin

kiwâpamâw cî oskâyaw ê-tapasît
wîkihk ôhci
iskotêwâpoy ê-tâkona
kaski tipsikâw
sisonê mêskanâhk ê-apit
ê-mamâtot tipiskahk

kiwâpamâw cî okâwîmaw ê-nîpawit
âpîhtâw nohtêkwasiw âpîhtâw âpisîkwasiw
pêyak osit iskwâhtemihk
pêyak ocîcî miciminam âsiyâniwat
nitotamawêw okiskinohamâkêma
têpiya pêyak kîsikaw

kiwâpamâw cî wîkimakan kâkwê pimacihot
ê-kanowsimwâkêk kwâmwâcisiwin
kîkâtowin
kâkwêyitamowin ascîkêmowin
konta asomisow ta-wanihisot

kiwâpamâw cî oksikinohamâkêw
awâsis mamitoneyicikan ê-sakâpihta
kâkwê micimâhpita
mâka mîkosowina
ohpaho makanwa

when you see me

do you see a little girl walking
with moshom
soft cree words blessing air?

do you see a teenager running
away from home
bottle of vodka in hand
blackout nights
sitting on the side of a road
crying in dark?

do you see a mother standing
half asleep—half awake
one foot in the door
one hand on a diaper bag
begging her teacher
for one more day?

do you see a wife weathering
under umbrellas of silence
storming arguments
jealous accusations
threatening to lose
herself?

do you see a teacher holding
kite strings of a child's mind
tying reason to ground
while gifts
catch wind and soar?

kiwâpamâw cî iskwêw ê-ayapit
sîpâ iykwaskwanoh
ê-nitoska tânisîsi kwayask
kêsi âcimot

kawâpamiyan niya
wâpamin niya

do you see a woman sitting
below rolling marshmallow clouds
searching for the right way
to tell her story?

when you see me
see me

kara onîmihitowin

nitô-kiskinohamâkê-minân
kitapinaw
itwêw
nimîk tâpiskohc akamâmak

samaskipayiw maskosî sîpâ pahkêkinêskisinihk
mâka namôya pikôpayiw
sâmiskamomakan askiy
kâwih ohpipayiw
pimihamakan
wêwêpipayiw akwanân
mitâtâkwanak ohpâsiwak
askitakwaw mihkwâw osâwaw wâpiskâw
miskâtikana wêwêpastanoh
misisi nêmisîsi
nawênam otitimana
nitohtawêw mistikwaskikwa
askiy opâhkahokowin

akwanân-isi-môwin itamwak
niya ohci kâkikê
kara onîmihitowin

cara's dance

she is our teacher
we sit—
she says
dance like a butterfly

grass bends under moccasin
but doesn't break
quickly touching ground
and up again
taking flight
fluttering shawl
wings catching wind
blue—red—yellow—white
fringe swaying
this way that
shoulders tip
ears focused on the drum
heartbeat of my land

they call it fancy
to me it is always
cara's dance

kipahikatêwa iskwahtêma

mihcêt pê-kipaham iskwahtêma
kiskêyitam ayisiyinwa ê-kâtâyit kîkway—kâya kitowêtâk
kîkway êkâ ê-wâpahta—namôya katahc takiskisit
okakêskîkêmow kostâ-nêtâkosiw
kimiyo wîcêtonâwâw cî
kôcipayitâw onaskomowin
ênêpêwihikot

wâpamonihk itâpiw—mâka nicipitam
ê-asawâpahta katawasisiwin
môskwêyitam mamitonêyitam nîpâtipisk
kîmôhc isi pîkiskwêw ispimihtakohk
kisâhkihin cî

yikatêyihtam âmwêyitamôwin—asamêw kîkisêpa onipêwiniyi
ê-kakwê kêcinâmat - namôya mamisi-wêyitâkosiw
kisiwêw—wîcipahpîmât kotaka nâpêwa
kiskânak
wâsaskotênam - pakamistikwânêsin wâsênamânihk
iskwêsapoy yasikawiniyiw ohkwâkanihk
wiyâkwêw kâya awiyak kawîhtamawat

nokwaniyiw oskîsikohk—namôya wiya otôcikan
kiyâm tanipaw
kotâka iskwêwa ocispakosiwiniyow
pasô
pîkôkâtêyiw okîci asocikêwin

konita itêyimikôwisiw—otîsâyâwin
kaskitêw masinâsiw oskîsikohk
nânâkatokêw oskana—wâpasakêw

behind closed doors

she's closed enough doors to know people have secrets
        shut out the noise
what she doesn't see—she doesn't have to remember

the counsellor's cold question
"how's your relationship with him?"
        she swallowed the answer
offended by its taste

she looked in mirrors—then tore them down
searching for beautiful
letting thoughts float away on tears in the middle of the night
        she whispered at the ceiling
"do you love me?"

she's pushed away doubt—served him breakfast in bed
        attempted to convince him—unpredictable him

she laughed too loud with another man
"slut"
white light—as her head hit window—beer cascading down her face
"don't fucken tell anyone"

insult in her eyes—it wasn't her fault
        let him sleep
while the stench of another woman
singed her nostrils—burnt her vows

she's suspicion's victim
        in her reflection
dark-circled eyes
studying bones
pressing skin white

kâkwê tapasistam
kîskwêpêw tipiskâwa—sîtikwêyiw—sîtâki-yawêw
ê-âsomiht cî âpoh ocîciyiw

pimpahtâw miyâskam cikastêsiniwin
acâkosak sâpo nôkosiwâk yikwaskanohk
tipiskâw-pîsimohk nôkwan mîhkwâkan
awasêwêw ê-ati sâkastêk
pakosêyitam ta wasêyâyik—matwân cî
tânêki kâkî-itêyita êwako sâkihitowin

she's trying to escape
drunk nights—cheeks pinched—spine rigid
was it the threat
      or the palm of his hand?

she's run past shadows—stars peeked through clouds
      the moon showed a face—turned and vanished into sunrise
she hungered for light
and wondered
why she ever thought that was love

ê-ati kîwêyân

êpasakwâpiyan wâyaw pêci nâway niwâhpahtên askiy mihcêt
miciminam mamaskahc kîkwaya nipê asê kiwênikon itê ênistawêy-
itamân pêyatikwêyimôwin nitakâkêyitên oski miskamowina

asinîs êwâsapiskisot nimêskwâpimâw mîna nimamitonêyitam yiyiko
êwîyôta nitaskiy—yitâmihk

ayîkihsak pêhtâkosiwak niwîhtamâkon ê-miyoskamik—tâkâpan
kâmiyo-tâkosicik piyêsîsak

kâkwâmwahci tipiskâk nimiyikon pêyâhtik takana-wahpahtamân
tânitawâpênamân nipawâtamôwina—mêscâkanis wanêwo-tam
kâkwâmwâtaniyik

kâpasoyân kimôwan nikiskisohikon nîpin—mwêstas kâ-misi kitocik
ê-pakamih-cîcêtotâkik kâ-ati mâyi kîsikâyik

nisâsâkîtin ê-ati miyaskamân kîkway kâ-miskamân kîsiwâw nikâwiy
askiy okaskitêw-asîskiy miciminam nitôcêpihkoma
nitaskiy miciminam nitehi nipê miskâson kîhtwâm kayâs âcimowini
sâkihitôwinihk mîna kâpâhpi nimiskên ita ê-ohciyan
kâpê âhkamêyimocik ê-kiskinota-mawicik sakihitowin manâcisowin
mîna kisêwâcisiwin miskikâtêw nanaskomôwini mîna atoskêwini

nôhkom kipimohtâtam oma asiskiy ê-asamât ôpâhpahâk-
wânima nikiskinohamâk tanisisi pimacisowin êyispayik mêkwahc
ê-wâsakâskâkot osit
nimôsom kî-pîkopitam askiy mitâtahtomtanaw askiya aspin mîna
tâyiwêpîhtât otayimihowina kêyapic nokwaniyow kistikanihk

ênitawi kiskisiyan êkoni kîsikâwa aspin wiyê—kâwi nimiyomâhcihon
ninikîhikwak nipihkôtamâkwâk mîwêyimowin okayaw-siyiniwa ôhci

homebound

closing my eyes I see a far off past—land holds many wonders—I
fall back on these comforts where familiarity brings me peace of
mind and I delight in youthful discoveries

how the sparkle of rock caught my eye and I imagined the riches of
my land—buried deep

when the melody of frogs told me that spring had come—its crisp
morning air—the harmony of birds

where the silence of night gave me time for contemplation to inves-
tigate my dreams—the simplicity broken only by coyote's howl

when the smell of rain reminded me of summer freshness—after the
loud claps of thunder applauded the passing storm

continuing past these findings I walk along barefoot—feel the
warmth of mother earth—her soft black dirt that holds my roots
my land holds my heart—I come back again to find myself in old
stories of love and laughter—I find my connection to family
their efforts to teach me that love—respect—kindness—founded in
thankfulness and hard work

nôhkom walked this same soil feeding her chickens—teaching me
about the cycle of life—as they clucked around her feet
nimôsom turned the packed earth one hundred years ago—and the
breadth of his struggles can still be seen in the dancing fields

reminiscing on days gone by—I feel the joys my parents brought me
from the fruits of their labor

nohtâwiy kistikêw okistikâni—pêyakoskanâw wâpakwaniya—
kistikêw oskâtaskwa napatâkwa mîna mâhtâmina—misi kistikêw
pahkwêsikanî kana

nikâwiy ayoskana—cîki êkôta—ayoskanâpoy atihtêwa nîpihta mîna
nitôn

nipê wâyinîn ita ê-ohciyân tawâhpahtamân pêyakwâw mîna
tapêyatikwêyimowin âsici acâhkosak

nipêtên nitaskiy nikamôwin—nikana-wapamawâk nicâpan-panak
nimîhitowak akwanâna oskaskosi mîna nîpâmayatan âkosiyiwa
kiwêtinohk ôcisimôwak

nipê kîwân nikiskisomison
niwîcêkon nitâskiy

my father sowing his crop—a row of lilies and roses—a garden of
carrots—potatoes—corn—a vast field of wheat
my mother's luscious raspberries—just a few steps away—where the
tangy red juices stained my lips and teeth

I come back to find solace in my history—to see the depth of the sky
once more—to fall away to peacefulness with the stars

I hear the song of my land—watch my ancestors as they dance in
shawls of purple and green across the northern sky

I come home again to remind myself
my land is with me

okanâta

niki-itakimikawin ayisînôw
1960
mâmitonê-yicikan mîna môsihowin
asici acâhk
ayamihêw-îniwak kîkakê otinamwâk
tâpiskôhc nitâskiy

pakwacâyi nikî-itikwâk
1982
ninêhiyawin
nitipêyimikon wiyasôwêwin
nitâskîhk

iyiniw
2007
kâkî kaskîtâyân tapi pimâcihisoyan
okimânâ ôhci
nitanwêw-tamâkawin
ta-wîhtaskêyimoyan

okanâta
tanispihk kakwayask-opayik

oh canada

declared me a human being
in 1960
with thoughts and feelings
with a spirit
missionaries had tried to claim
like my land

called me an aboriginal
in 1982
I am nêhiyaw
with undefined rights
to my land

an indigenous person
in 2007
with the right to self-determination
despite a government
denying legal obligation
to share my land

oh canada
when will you get it right?

icisahamawâw masinahikan onîkaniw dan george

ham onîkaniw
ispihk ê-ayitiyin
nêhiyaw nikî itikawin
kiya yiyiniw kikî isin
miyo kîsikâw
tanakataskê

kikî mîhtâtên wîtaskânêtowin
pîkiskwêwin pê-mawîkâcikâtêw
awîna namôya cêskwa mawîhkâtam
kâkî wanîtâya askiy

kikîskisominan
namôya takawaho sîtak
êkâ ê-kâkîsimoh
kinohsêwâk piko takanataniyik nipiy
tôpikihitocik
pêyak kinosêw otinâw takanawâpamiht
kôtawêyitam kîcikamihk

kikî-masinahên kîkway kâkî pawâtaman
kikî-âyimôtên pêci-nâwayi
kikî pakosêyimon kosisimâk
namôya cêskwa ênîtâwikicik

a letter to chief dan george

dear chief
in your time they called me indian—you called me a human being
it was a good day
to die

your "lament for confederation"—words that cried tears for generations
who had not yet mourned
for a land lost
to big timber companies

you reminded us
red cedar should not be chopped without prayer
racing salmon need clean rivers to spawn
shy orca caught and put on show
misses the open waters of the sea

you wrote about your dreams—you spoke about the past
looked forward to grandchildren
not yet born

I miss your smile—your wisdom
the way your poetry
made me feel human

they called me indian
in your time

nikôta wêyitên ki-pâhpîwikwêwin
kitî-yiyinîsiwin
kâkî isi mâsinahikêyin
nikî miyo ayisiyiniw-mâhcihon

nêhiyaw nikî itikawin
ispîhk ê-âyitiyin

ita kâ-âyîtiyan
nitaysînimak pêkopayiwâk
anohc êkwa kinisitôtâtin
osâm nitacâhk nikamôw
nitehi ôpahomakan
mîna kâkikê
miyo kîsikâw
tanakataskê

but in my time
my people awakened
now I understand you—because my spirit sings
my heart soars
and it is always
a good day
to die

askiy
———
Land

itâpi

mîtos namôya kostam
ta mêskocît

ispihk ê-kisipwêk
wâskwapoy pimiciwan
mâci sâkihpakâw
piyisk nîpiya nôkwanoh
otinam sâkâstêw mîna
nipayastêw

kwêkwêskâso miyikîsikâ
takwâkiyawêw
mêskocinâkwnoh nîpiya
oskaskosîwâwa osâwâwa,
mîna mikosâwâwa
wêwepâstanoh kâ yôtik

mîtos wâwâstahikêw
kakwêskinâkwaki nîpiya
pêyatik
wî pipon
pakitinam
mitosâcikos namoya miciminam pinipakaw

katapowakêyitami
kâwi ta kisipwêw

look

the tree is not afraid
to change

when warmth embraces bark
sap runs
bud shoots and curls
twisting open into leaf
soaks up sunrise
receives each moon
flips unrest in storms

when days grow short
damp autumn air
displaces green
smears yellow
paints orange
swaying in cutting gusts

the tree
proudly waving
the colours of caution
predicting winter
letting go
no stem clings to falling leaf

winter is worn with trust
that warmth will reemerge

nâtawihowin

nohtâwiy âtotam kîkway êkîhiki
ispîhk nicâpan
kîkiskêyitam kîkwaya kitaskînahk
namôya maskîkîwiyiniw omaskîkîma
namôya ôhci masinahikâtêw nâtawihowin
kîkiskêyitam nâtawihowina
nîpîhk
kâwîsakahk
kâwîhkasik wîhkask
okini-wâpakwanî
wiyâpôkan kâwîsakahk mîna kâwîhkasik
maskêko ohpikin
wâsakam sâkahikani

kîwîsâmêw nisikosa pêyakwâw
ta kiskinohamawât
mâka pîtos âskiywin
wanitâw ta-kiskisit
masinahikan ayimîcikêwin
pahkêkin-owata

êkâ nicapan
takiskinohtahit
ita kapimohtêyân oma askiy
nikitîkapimawak okiniyak
nikiskêyitên
kâhkiyaw kîkway tâpacihikoyân
kâsômakan
nitaskihk

medicine

my father speaks of a time
when great grandmother
knew the secrets of our land
no doctor drugs
no pen for prescriptions
knowledge of the medicine
folded in the leaves
of stinging nettle
sweet sage
wild rose
teas both bitter and sweet
growing in the mucky muskeg
around the lake

she took my aunt out once
to teach her
but an unwelcoming world
faded memories
with school books
leather straps

without my great grandmother
to guide me
walk this land
flushed rosehips catch my eye
I know
everything I need
is hidden
in the secrets of my land

kanawâpamâtanik piyêsîsak

kaskitêw âhasiw yînto mîtosi akasiw
kisiwêw ê-kitot
nohtê nâkatohâtikosiw

askîtako piyêsîs akosiw
êkâsot
nâway oskâtakâ

waskahikan piyêsîs sâsamaskipihow
tâpiskohc kapatahikêmaka mososinî
kwêkwêskakocin

kitowê-tâtakwan piyêsîs wâpakwanisa sôpahtam
âsê-pihaw kawi pêsôpahtam kîhtwam
nohtê-yâpâkwêtotam kâ-wîkasiniyik

kêkahc mêscihaw ocicâk nipawiw
maskêkohk pâhkopêw
ayiwêpow yikatawâ

mistêyimisiw niska êpimikitot
atamiskakêw
ê-pimikîwêt itê ê-otaskît
mosci nistawêyitam

kîci kihiw apisci-nâkosiw
wâyaw ispimihk ê-pimihat
sawêyitam kîsikâw

taniyiko ê-nistawêyitocik

bird watching

old black crow sits high in poplar
laughing loudly
his ego begs attention

masked blue jay perches
shying from sight
behind branches of tamarack

swift sparrow swoops
like a stray bullet off-target
spinning left to right

darting hummingbird dips in buds
backing up—dips again
thirsty for sweetness

endangered crane stands
feet buried in muskeg
resting in slough

proud goose honks past
a farewell
migrating to a destination
known only by heart

great bald eagle a tiny dot
weaving in the highest skies
blesses the day

how well do they know each other?

osôwâskwa

âstêsinômakan
yîtatêyitamôwin
âpo êtikwê anohc

pasikôpitam askihk ôhci
sîtawâstâw mîpiti
wâpiski asapapis oskaskosîwa
miyomawisiw capasis ospiskwani
sâsîh-pîhkêyita

awas
niwîkatêtawâwak osakimêsak
tânika yôtik
nitapwêsiwin yiyasikawin niskâtikohk
sâsîh-pîhkêyita

wîkatê sîkwatam miscikos
paskopitam kotak ta mîcit
yiyâyinam kawâpiskayik
tânisi êtikwê êtâpata
sâsîh-pîhkêyita

nuh
itwahikêw sisonê sakahk
tâkohc pâkwêsikanî-kânihk
tâkohc maskosihk
osôwaskwa
wâpiski asapâpi-nâkwanwa

mawomosiwâk acimosisak
pôni pêhowin

foxtails

lulls of time
anticipation
maybe today

plucked from earth
placed between teeth
white tassels on green stalk
damp warmth below back
patience

awas!
swatted mosquitoes
wanted wind
perspiration drops on my hairline
patience

spat the chewed stem
plucked another morsel
ran my fingers through the tassel
what purpose did they serve?
patience

nuh!
pointed towards the brush line
above wheat
above the brush of grasses
foxtails
white-tipped tassels

whimper of pups
wait is over

wâsaka-tâpâsowin

môcikan
paskwa
mêskanâhkânisi
mwêtas niso
kîsikawa ê-kî-kimôwa

rollercoaster

the thrill
on prairies
a grid road
after two
days of rain

paskwâwo-mostosomina

mîhko-kîkânâkwanwo
oskaskosîwanohk
nipimipahtân
nîpisîsa
nêscakâsi akwamonwa
nipâhkisinin
natâ
shhhhh
nikostên
oswoy
nimâmakatâtên
nikasêkihaw
misatim ê-otêskanit
apisimôsos
yiyâkîtâp niwîcêwâkan

ohpahow pîsim ê-ati pônakoci
paskwâwo-mostosomina
kîkânâkwanwo
oskaskosîwanohk
nikiskisin
                    mamaskâhc ispayiwina takiskisihk

buffalo berries

red glow
amongst green
I run
branches whip
cling to my hair
then down
my stomach on earth
Shhhhh!
I fear
her thumping tail
panting tongue
will scare away
unicorn
deer
elfin friend

late august
buffalo berries
glow
amongst green
I remember
            adventures

kîkwaya ê-pêkiskêyitamân

wâyawês
namôya kîkway pêtâkwan kakwâmwâtan
wanwêkamwâk hâhâsowâk ê-kitocik
nîpiya kitowêyâstanwa
nikiskêyitên
sâmiskitômakwanwa nîpiya
êwîmêskocowêpa
naspâtakotêwa nîpiya mitosihk
wîmâyikîsikaw

nîpisîwatik
nânawêyasiw yotinohk
oskâtakwak
osâwâskwanwa
misiwêskâw

kihiw kitôw
wâwâsakâpihaw
otâtâkwana wastahikâkêw
yotin niyâkiwêpahok nispiskwani
nikiskêyitên
ta kîwêyan

what I learned

far enough away
nothing but silence
interrupted by laughing crows
and the wind flipping leaves
I learned
leaves brush each other
give a murmur of weather approaching
leaf rapping upside down against a tree
a storm

weeping willow
bows to wind spirits
golden tamaracks
cloak buttery clouds
smear the sky

eagle shrieks
traces a figure eight
wings on waves
wind thrusts my back
I learned
to go home

pâpâkwêcakêsîs

ki-nihkamon
ki nîmihtân âskiwihwin
rat-a-tat-tat
mistikohk
ki-yêyîtân ê-isi mâtwêhikêyin
kâkitwân ki-matwêtahikân
ê-yispi-sî-yin
ta-nawaswêyin kitâ-cimowin
ê-yisi mîkôwsiyin

woodpecker

your song
is the hiphop of nature
rat-a-tat-tat
against a wooden drum
provocative beat
repetitive rap
lyrically inclined
to follow your poetic
genius

kâkitowak

boom
cistâwêmâkan misiwê niyaw

namôya nisêkisin

wâni-nâkwan
âci kamêscipayiw kâ-pawâtaman

namôya nisêkisin

takâkimâkwanwa maskosiya
kâkîsi kimôwa wantipiskâ

namôya nisêkisin

thunderstorm

boom
vibrates in every chasm of my body

I am not afraid

twisted light
threatens to burn every dream tonight

I am not afraid

sweet scent
rain on grass in the dark

I am not afraid

nohtâwiy asinîwaciy

ita kayâs sîpiy
ê-mâcicôwa
kôna tâkohc akocin
maskosîwaskâ
tâtakwâcâ
wâwâ-kotêciwan
isko nîkihk

father mountain

where ancient river
starts the journey
from snowcap peak
to grassland field
carving valleys
winding its way
to my home

tâtakwâca pêhtâkosiwâk

mâmatwêkikêwak
pêtâkosiwak askihk
asiskî wohpastêw akopayiw
nânawatinam pîhkohowin
atîtâpawêw kisipaskî
mâyi-kîsikanaskwâw
tâtakoskam
pâhpotâ-cikêw
kostâ-nacâpo

nâciyoscikêw omâciw
sisonê sakâhk
cistahaskwâkan nêpêminam
askiy koskoskopayiw
kîskimiyawêw
pêhtâw kaminahot
kawîhkokânaw anohc kâtipiskâk
kôsîtânaw wâskahikan
nanâskomotân
kisâstê

prairie thunder

pounding hooves
thunder on earth
dust rising—clinging
gasping at freedom
washing over the horizon
a pregnant storm cloud
trampling
sage and sweetgrass
flaring nostrils
frantic eyes

creeping hunter peers
from brush line
spear pointed
ground shaking
vertebrae vibrating
anticipation of the kill
we will feast tonight
make tools
house our families
give thanks
in the hot sun

mêscâkanis

yip yip
aaaaaoooooooooo
kiwiyoyon

nitasêkwêyin
kinaskomitin
kaskêyitam tipiskâw
êka-kwamwâta

yip yip
aaaaaoooooooooo
kiwiyoyon

ati pêhtâkwan
pîkâciskîtâkwan nikamon

mêscâkanis

yip yip
aaaaaoooooooo

tilting my head back
returning your call
fills many lonely nights
of prairie silence

yip yip
aaaaaoooooooo

trailing off
in sorrowful song

pîhkohowin

kîkway nikanawâpamik
wâpistikwânêw
akosîw minahikohk
wîposâwisiyiwa omîkwana
akwanaham wâsiskan
wâsakam pimâtan hêhêwin
pîkâcisistâkosiw mâkwa
kinosêwak kwâskwê-pahihowâk sâkahikanihk
kîkway otîtinam kôtâkwan mîcisot
wâyiniw owatastwanihk
wîhkôkêw

ati-otâkosin
asiniy-wacihk âkawaskwêw
okinî-wâpakwaniw-nakwan nipîhk
wâkayos tapê-wâyiniw
ocîcipayin ta-sipwêtêyân
miyaskawâwak okiniyak
pakwaci wâpakwaniya
cikâsipakwa
yoskâcaw askiya mêskanasi
ê-sipwêtahit
ohci pîhkohowini

freedom

stranger watches me
bald white head
perches in evergreen shade
curtain of cocoa-colored feathers
shawl wraps chest
around us the air is alive
loon calls sadness
fish jumps in sapphire lake
stranger snatches his supper catch
returns to his nest
feasts

evening settles in shadows
mountains block sunset
pink tinge on water
bear will return soon
time to go
past rosehips
wild orchids
kinnikinnick
spongy moss path
taking me away
from freedom

isko nipiy ta-pimihciwa

nikâwiy omîhko nimihkwêyapihk pimiciwân
atâmaskihk pimiciwân nipiy
wâsakam kiskinoham wâhkôtowin
piscipôtâwak ayisîniwak

nikâwiy
nitâkonik ê-nôhit
kakêtâ-wihsiwin

nikâwiy
o-pâhkikawâpowin
kâsîpêpayow kônihk kâ-oski-pâhkisi

kayâs onikâniw kipîkiskwata asotamâtowin
isko pîsim ka wâsisot
maskosî tôpiki
mîna nipiy ta-pimiciwa

nikâwiy omîhko nimihkwêyâpîhk pimiciwân
atâmaskihk pimiciwân nipiy
wahwa-niciwan pimâtisiwin êmîkowisi
piscipôtâwak ayisîniwak

as long as the waters flow

my mother's blood flows in my veins
water rushing underground
circling—mapping a path to my relations
poisoned by men

my mother
cradling me as I pull at her breast
feeding me knowledge

my mother
her cold tears falling
erased in the purity of fresh fallen snow

an old chief spoke at treaty
as long as the sun shines
the grass grows
and the waters flow

my mother's blood flows in my veins
water rushing underground
twisting—coiling into life-giving currents
poisoned by men

nitacâhkosim

pêyak ayiwâk wâsisô
pêyak astawênêw kotaka
nitacâhkosim
wâsiso wâsakamê
tânisi tohtamihitê êmisi tawâk
mêskanahk-âtam wânêyitamowin
tapônipayihtâk namôya kêcinâhowin
nitacâhkosim
nanâto itâsowêw
nitacâhkosim
wâsisô âpîhtâ-tipiskâ
pâhpîwîkwêwin môsinakwan

my star

one brighter than the rest
one makes others fade away
my star
light crosses
fathoms of space
navigates confusion
shoots at insecurity
my star
ignites colours
my star
blazes across midnight dark
glimpse of a smile

sikwan

ah ha
kitô hahâsiw
ayîkisak kitôwak
yôcinis nikâsîkwênik
wêwêpasiwak mîtosâk
tâkohc nipêhtawâwak osakimêsak
cistêmâw nipakitinaw
ita oskaskosî ê-pênôkwa
ninanâskotên miyoskamin

sikwan

ah ha
cries crow
frogs sing
breeze washes my face
budding trees waltz
mosquito clouds hum above me
I place tobacco
where green shoots begin to show
welcome spring

ôski kîsikâw

wâpan
mihko pêsonakwan itê askiy êkwa kisik kanakiskâtocik
nitoskawêw tipiskâwpîsimwa

mihkwasi-nastêwa yikwaskwanoh
misiwê kîsik

mîtosak osawi cikâstêsinok
askiy

takosino-makan
nîpâ nawaso cikastêtin
kwamwâtaskwaw kîsik

osâwâsinastêw askiytakwâ
kâmiyikowisiya

a new day

daybreak
red breaches horizon
hunting the moon

bloodshot
scarlet streaks clouds
smearing the sky

silhouette
gold coats black trees
edging the land

arrival
mauve chases shadow
calming heavens

crowning
orange blushes on blue
presenting the gift

sasîpihtamô awâsisak

nêkâ nimihtâtên
nikiskêyitên namôya mistahi itêyitâkwan
nitapisîsin ninêsôwâtisin
aspin kâpê-ociyân kipê pamihin
kâhkiyâw kîkwaya nitawêyitamani

nipêhtên kipîkiskâtêyimowin yôtinohk
niwâpahtên kiwîsakêyitamowin piponohk
nipêhtên kikisiwâsowin misi-mâyikîsikahk
nimôsîtân kikaskêyitamowin
tawanisikik kitawâsimisâk
niwâpahtên kisêkisiwin
ta wanihsikihk
kikisîw kitohtâwâk sasîpihtamô awâsisak
kosikwan cîciya ki-pakahmahokon

nêkâ nimihtâtên
pônêyitamawin

disobedient children

mother—I am sorry
I know that doesn't mean much
I am small and weak
and you have provided for my every need
since the first day broke your horizon

I hear your sorrow in the wind
I see your pain in brown of winter
I hear your anger in violent storms
I feel your grief
ruin of your children
I see your fear
shaking and crashing
land against land
scolding disobedient children
heavy hands beating on you

mother—I am sorry
pardon my insolence
I will change

nêwo wiyasowêwina

misiwê askiy iyiniwak-ayitiwak
nêwoyak ê-yispihtaskamikak wiyasowêwina

kitimâkêyitowin
okâwîmâw kanawâpamêw otâkonawasôwina
otî-yikicîcân miciminamiyow
kanawâpahtowâk asotâmawin nistawi-nâtowak
nistohcikâtên

tâpwêwin
wîcisânimâw namôya pêhtawâw
kâhkihtwâm wihtam ayihtowin
namôya awiyak nohtê pêhtam
mâka piko ta-wihtami

manâcisowin
ohtâwîmâw napakiskawêw kaminakasiya
namôya natwaskawêw
tamanâcity pakwaci ayitiwin
macikwanâs namôya nitawêy-icikatêw pisikistikanihk

nanâskomowin
pêyak ospwâkan cistêmwa awâsis pakitinêw
nipisîw wacêpîhkohk
ka nanâskota kanawisihmowin

kiwâpahtên
nitati kiskêyitên

four laws

"there are four universal laws
in indigenous cultures around
the world"

love
a mother's eyes upon her baby
finger clasped in tiny hand
a look—a promise—a recognition
understood

honesty
a sister's words beating deaf ears
rhythmically repeating reality
nobody wants to hear
but must be said

respect
a father's step on thistle
bending not breaking
to protect purpose of wild
weeds unwanted in garden

thankfulness
a child's fingers pinch tobacco
sacred grass of offering
placed around the roots of willow
for protection

do you see?
I am learning

asiniy

sîpîwâsiniy
soskwâpawêw
âcimowina kikiyawâtên
tânisi êyisi wawocik kinosêwak
notinamwak wiyawa-tikociwan
nitonamwak katawi-kamâyik

sîpîwâsiniy
wâpiskisiw tâkisiw maskawisiw
oci kanawâpahtam
kikiyawâtam kayâs âcimowina
wîkohkêwina

tâpiskohc sîpîwâsiniy
nisoskonatikon
yiyinîsowin
matwân cî

stone

the river stone
smoothed by water
etched with stories
of spawning salmon
fins fighting current
looking for vast open water

the river stone
white—cold—hard
is the watchful eye
holding history
carrying ancient ceremony

like the river stone
have I been smoothed
etched with knowledge
I wonder

tâtwâw kâ kimôwa

kâkî simonânawiw
nistam oskîsikwâpoy
oskawâsis

namôya awiyak nôhkom tawîhtamawit
maskîkîwiyiniw piko

maskîkîwiskwêwâk wêwêkinêwak tipâpêskôhêwâk
piyisk nitâkonâw
kêyapic ohcikâwâpow

namôya nikiskêyitên tâtôtamân
namôya kîkway miyâkasikan

mâka tâhtwâw kâ-kimôwa
kâsamas-kâpâwêki nîpiya

niwâpahtamwân oskîsikwâpoy
sawêyimikôwisiw

every time it rains

there is a ceremony
for the first tears
of a newborn

there is no kokom to tell me
only doctors
with beeping machines
nurses swaddle and weigh him
at last he's in my arms
water still clutches the corners
of his eyes

no smudge, no connection
unknowing what to do

but every time it rains
tapping drops against
blades of grass
leaves bending heavy
I see his tears
water
bestowed